My AttiTude

a book of hope by

Maurine Fergueson

illustrations by

Brad Hayes

Noble House
Baltimore, Maryland

My AttiTude

Illustrations by Brad Hayes

Library of Congress
Cataloging in Publication Data
ISBN 1-56167-305-6

Library of Congress Card Catalog Number:
96-068092

Published by

Noble House

8019 Belair Road, Suite 10
Baltimore, Maryland 21236

Manufactured in the United States of America

I dedicate this book to my family
because they didn't think I could
"Do It."

Table of Contents

God's Orientation

Is it time yet God, for my earth mission? A stalemate now is my Spirit's condition. I want to get on, with my eternal journey, and advance one more step, of necessary learning.

My child, you are ready, to change your abode. Where you are going only faith, will your mind hold. Every now and then, you will know Deja Vu. It could be more than once, this portal you go through.

There are many things, that could stunt your stay. You won't come back until, you've gone all the way. Only I know how far you must go, and when you are ready to come back to the fold.

You may not like how your spirit's enclosed. When you return you will know why, this flesh I chose. There are deeds of others that can change the form that I chose for you on the day you are born.

Your body could be severed, before the day you inhale. It doesn't mean your entrance has failed. I am God, and I say what will be. You will breathe Earth's air by another entry.

I know all the things your spirit requires. Every breath's been recorded, before you expire. Once your spirit's been filled with atmosphere, it could be only a second before you are back here. You will have achieved one of the ground rules. Your spirit doesn't need, any of life's schools.

There are many talents, and I will bless you with some. You might live a long time and never recognize one. You will be confused and frustrated, and want to know why you can't excel, or get out what's deep inside.

You might rebel at the peak of your glory, or have to abandon it because you feel poorly. Maybe your best work will just have to wait for immediate chores that you can't forsake. You could reveal your artistic talent, at a very young age. Then it won't be a burden to go on to another stage.

Your talent might not be to bring great pleasure, or to get admiration and obtain earthly treasure. Your talent could be a simple daily chore you do over and over, until you are bored. The world may never notice how you've endured, and your keep will be the one to get what you deserved.

If you cared enough to get the seeming trifle things done, I will know you belong to my Monarch ones. You were blessed with a talent not rare. Very few will embrace, your effort to care.

Your appearance might not be the perfection you want. The perception on earth is of Human nature that taunts. Your spirit's remittent to see only the shore. Whatever's beyond, you will have to study and explore. There will be renegades who will be the sender and only from some, resentment they will render. The actions caused by insults will be a mixture of results. Some will derive and precipitate a terrible wrong. Some will invent a soul saving song.

Some of My spirits will be endowed with an outward beauty. This will be coveted and wanted without fulfilling any duty. They will say on earth, "Don't judge a book by its cover." Read it so you can honestly discover if the beauty or ugliness goes to the core. Then if you want to understand more, seek the author if they can be found. If it doesn't impress you, put it down.

Each spirit is anxious, that's why they are not shown, the chaos that is part of their earth home. You will be born with a conscious intact. How it is developed will depend on Human acts. You will know like an animal to get out of the rain. To find a safe shelter, you will have a brain. If your conscious is good, you will bring the animal inside. If it's dormant and nil, only you will be safe and dry.

There is plenty for all, if they will share, but it's one

of the decisions I placed in their care. Many don't own any worldly goods. Some wouldn't possess them even if they could. Many acquire riches galore. Many of them would rather die than be poor.

There is nothing on earth your spirit can use, except for the knowledge, all else, I will refuse. When you return to continue your journey, you will need only the lessons and bonding to continue through eternity.

There's something on earth you've never known here. There are many reasons for the emotion called Fear. It will be a deterrent to prevent fatal mistakes. Also a protective weapon to keep you alert, when you are awake.

Sometimes fear will be a challenge to overcome. There will be times the source is unwarranted, fear comes from. You will rarely know total peace because fear and regret will never cease. It's good and it's bad, but it tops my list, for the emotions you need to exist.

Hate is the emotion you must fight to tame. If you let it run rampant, your soul it will claim. Anger, revenge, envy, greed, evil, all breed in hate's name. Hate will pester you to play its fatal game, because when you win, your reward will be shame. More often than not, you can't redeem Grace again.

The most powerful feelings, your spirit will learn, and I hope it will master you when you return. It's the Mother of Peace and Joy, and Eternal Light. When you feel love, you will know everything that's right.

Love can capture a will, that's gone wrong, and courageously place it where it belongs. It can hold back the tide from any Sea, and even bring Me to My knees. In the name of love, whatever you do, will be carried on with a heart that's true.

There will be many who claim, love is their mate. If it isn't worthy, it's greed, revenge, or hate. Love can be masked and falsely accused. Many times it will be terribly abused. Love is very fragile and hurts when it is refused.

You should never expect love to be returned in kind. The interpretation is as individual as the mind. Let it flow freely, but prevent a flood. You don't want to smother anyone that is loved.

Most of all love comes from within. The core of your heart is where it will begin. Your heart will beat, and the blood will flow through your veins. Your spirit, most of all, will absorb love's refrains. You may or may not possess those you love, but the spirit will return with the knowledge above.

Sometimes you will curse me, when you lose or destroy something you built. The burning and pain is your feelings of guilt. It's all right, because I know how helpless you feel. I hope you will leave your soul out of your appeal.

Many actions on Earth will be viewed with alarm. The worst will be accepted, because a disguise is worn. You'll have only the power to hear, touch, see and smell. Some bodies will lose or lack senses that I tell. Your spirit will be bound by your body's shape, and your mind will weaken the wisdom of what it takes.

The church's on Earth are flowers in My Garden. They will help you achieve a Diocese pardon. While on Earth that's all you will need. I've already forgiven every sinful deed.

All through your life, you will be burdened with pride. You'll want the whole world, to know you are alive. You'll want to be first, and always the best. For this glory on Earth, you will never rest.

If your mate is the one who is admired and praised, or it could be a child you have dutifully raised. No matter the reason, a light shines on you, your heart will feel joy and your pride will too. An inward pride for a job well done is the richest of all under Heaven's Sun.

If you perpetrate a terrible wrong, or someone you love has failed to be strong. If you endure and accept the inflicted pain, then you can be proud in spite of the shame. All that happens on Earth, good or bad, will fall on My name. My Being understands and can stifle the blame.

Faith is not a feeling your body or Earth, can instill. It's part of your spirit, it's called your own will. You may try to deny faith, as many have and will do. It is eternal because, I give it to you.

Life after death will always be a mystery. The truth will be sought, all through History. This is one secret, no Human form will ever be shown. When life gets unbearable, you will go on, because you fear the unknown.

You won't consciously remember any of this. You will always know there is something you miss. You will be searching on Earth for Heavenly Bliss. The Kin on Earth, is a gentle Kiss.

The spirit was appalled, and filled with revere, as out of God's Eye fell a new born Tear.

Material or Spiritually, Rich or Poor

There is a major difference, in material rich or poor and spiritually, rich or poor.
If the quality, not the quantity, of life was measured, who would have more?

If you are rich as a King, but have no peace of mind, because you think someone's richer, or could steal your Gold mine.

Or the Homeless who holds some bread in his hand.
And breaks it in half, to share with another man.

Are you exulted, looking at all you survey?
Or content to have shelter at the end of the day?

Jesus was known to have spent his time, among the material poor.
He might have found his teaching just as needed on a rich man's shore.

It's a pitiful sight to see someone in need.
They might just be lazy, or lost all through greed.

You can give and give to some people who are poor.
They will squander and manipulate, keep coming back for more.

There are people who obtain riches with deceit and force.
There are rich people who work hard and are honestly endorsed.

Your obvious station in life never reflects your true need.
In a mansion or on the street, if you're cut, you bleed.

You could be poor in the knowledge to heal your wound.
Rich or poor you need a teacher to save you from Doom.

I'm absolutely sure, there is a superior Being
Who sees and knows all, doesn't miss a thing.

If you are rich or poor, that Being doesn't care.
You are judged as Humans, if it's Rags or Riches you wear.

Humans have many reasons for good and bad, as there are grains of sand. And God holds each reason, in the palms of His hands.

Thou shall not kill, thou shalt not steal, is not aimed at only the least of us.
The Widow, the Orphan, the Sport hero, the Entertainer, the King, all need Spiritual guiding and Human Trust.

If you are poor, your body can die because of hunger or violence. If you are rich, your spirit can die from lonely, unyielding silence.

Rich or poor, your body and spirit can become null.
When tragedy strikes, a teacher is needed by all.
A Tale I will tell, because it's impossible to decide,
What a Human holds, until you've seen inside.

GAZETTE
EXAMINER
BRAD HAYES

The Beggar and the King

If a King is sick, a Beggar could be the only one who has the remedy.
It's up to the Beggar to relieve and get paid, or do it for free.

If the Beggar requests that his family always be fed,
And the King replies, "I will, until I am dead."
The Beggar said, "If I die first, can I depend on your word?
You might be a King, but not a very good one, I've heard."

The King very puzzled said, "Why did you help me when the truth you knew?"
The Beggar shrugged. "Because, it's the right thing to do."

The King humbly said, "Will you and your family come and live in my palace,
So you can guide me and teach me, to live without malice?"

So the King helped the beggar, but not because the Beggar saved the King.
The King was wise enough to recognize, the way to redeem.

The Beggar and his family, forever, had the King for their Host.
The Beggar went to town everyday to Beg because that's what he loved the most.

The Beggar's wife taught the Kingdom to love, and the children filled it with laughter.
Because someone did the right thing, the rich and the poor lived happily ever after.

If you wanted to save, and on a mission you were sent,
Out of the Beggar and the King, which one was meant.

It's very unfair to refuse help because one is wealthy,
Or they are beautiful, or smart, or extremely healthy.

And if you see a Beggar out on the street,
Who is a pitiful sight, no shoes on his feet.
It just might be the life that he chose.
Material poorness isn't the worst of life's woes.

To be poor is to be worthy of pity or sympathy.
Rich means superior in quality, or material riches, in
great quantity.

I asked God, as I squeeze
Out a tear,
Do I have to go? I'm happy
here.
He puffed up his chest, looked
Me straight in the eye,
Then He relaxed, shook his head,
And let out a sigh.
He put my hand in His. "I love you,
Sweet child. It's time for your birth.
I'll always be near to help the
Others you encounter on Earth."

Was He Here?

There are lots of gods to help people feel their worth.
I've been wondering, was God here on Earth?

Does he know what it's like when the dark causes fear?
Or get punished or lost, and shed a tear?

Did He feel envy when someone had it all?
Did He spill His milk, or trip and fall?

Does He know what it's like to fall in love?
Or watch the snow softly drift down from above?

Did He work long hours without a break?
Did His stomach or His teeth, or His head, ever ache?

Does He know what it's like to have His feelings hurt?
Or get up in the morning and have to iron His own shirt?

Did He stand in a soup line, when He was hungry and cold?
Did He lose His eyesight or hearing when He grew old?

Was He ever sorry for something He did?
Or have to ask someone, to please forgive?

Was He ever in a foxhole, afraid to raise His head?
Or homeless and begging, a park bench, for His bed?

He couldn't have set forth all the rules
If He didn't experience all of life's schools.

If this is true, when He put us down here,
I know for a fact, He always, stays near.

It's Simple to Me

Religion is based on evil and superstition.
God doesn't make us search for His tradition.

God didn't give His instructions to one, to be a mystery.
So the rest would fight and search, all through History.

We are so busy searching and wanting the true God,
But any material object will be a fraud.

An ark, a book, a robe, a person, an idol, there are many.
Just look around you, False Prophets are plenty.

There are people who will give, money and their life.
Because some person says, " My way is right."

God doesn't want money, or you to fight for His love.
He doesn't look down and judge us from above.

God isn't hiding, so don't waste your time.
There are no secrets or miracles for you to find.

There are no ceremonies, or rites, you have to perform.
We are all known to God the day we are born.

God's dimensions are eternal and flawless. His existence complete.
He can govern the Universe. He knows us. He doesn't have to seek.

I know kids are always searching for their fathers on earth,
But our Heavenly Father stays with us from birth.

Can you love a leader who uses threats to make you obey,
Or one who understands you have to be wrong to find the right way?

Can you imagine a God who plays a silly game of hide and seek,
When His wisdom and beauty surrounds us if you're brave or meek.

God doesn't give His blessings to a chosen few.
Man's arrogance and pride, makes him believe, that's what God would do.

If God wants the black sheep, to join the fold,
Then why do church's excommunicate when we don't do what we are told?

When we are bad, God doesn't say, "Get out of here."
Each time anyone is punished, God sheds a tear.
He knows it's a necessity while we are here.

And when one of God's does a hideous crime, God cushions the victim's pain and clouds their mind.

My mom used to say, "If you're rich, and everything's fine,
The Devil's already got you, with you, he doesn't have to spend any more time."

You can deny God, search for him, argue his reality or cry, He isn't fair.
God won't punish you, hate you, no matter how long you've searched, He's always been there.
When things get real bad, tell God it's His turn to care.
Because He did promise you, He wouldn't give you more than YOU could bear.

I Protest

It's not easy to be humble,
Especially when your efforts crumble.
And most of all, when you are not sincere,
Because you really don't feel like
Your students are peers.
Why do I have to stoop to a mindless level,
And welcome the tactics of the devil?
I open my arms to embrace what is wrong,
To bless the sinner with a humble song.
I can't be part of the soul saving crowd.
Forgive me God, I protest, clean and loud.

The Voice Within, The International Society of Poets

The Wandering One

I was tending my flock, and one wandered away.
I needed to leave, and bring home the stray.

What would I do with the rest in my care?
Who would tend to their needs if I wasn't there?

If I stay with the rest, and ignore this one,
In time all might leave, then I'd have none.

Will they all stay here if I leave them alone,
To go out and bring back one of their own?

Will they wonder what's out there, if they take the same
path? Or will they be content, if I bring the wandering
one back?

First, I must learn why one was compelled to take,
This path. Was it inquisitive nature, or an ultimate
escape?

I'll reverently study the rest of my flock.
I won't be aloof, among them, I will walk.

If I find one more, I think I will lose,
I'll give them all, the right to choose.

I don't want to demand and control my keep.
I want them to earn and believe in what they reap.

So I've decided to just wait and see,
If the rest will stay, and the wandering one will come
back to me.

I sing a song,
Of God and love.
My voice is strong
With truth, not fraud.
They say to me,
"Be silent" now.
You are not free
To kneel or bow.
Some others complain,
you offend.
Your words are pain
To a mortal friend.

The Right End of the Line

I got distracted, and stepped out of the line.
It happened again, like it does every time.
I know to acquire most anything, you have to wait.
Stand for hours and hours, holding your plate.
And anytime you get side tracked
You have to walk, clear to the back.
The spot where you stood closes in real fast.
Then you find yourself, once again, being last.
Nature calls, a meal is due, nothing can wait.
Except what you want, for a later date.
I'm tired of standing in that stupid old line,
To get almost there, and then to find,
I can't stay put, I'll lose my place,
All of that effort, has gone to waste.
It's something I want. It's only for me.
If only the rest of the world could see.
I'm not around just to wait on them,
Be a wife, a mother, a maid, a cook, a friend.
I'm demanding now, you step out of the way.
I'm standing in line, and I won't even sway.
Well here I am, right at the front.
And the person there says, "I hate to be blunt.
This isn't the line, you should have stood in.
I kept throwing you out, but you'd come back again.
This is the line where life's race is won.
And there were too many things you had to get done.
But if you feel you have completed all of life's chores,
I will take you in, and give you your rewards.
But know that the ones, you left behind,
Are standing now, in the same wrong line.
If you think, they can make it without you,
Don't worry about them, come on through.
But, if you have doubts and want to do more,
You can go back before you go through the door.

You can show them, they're in the wrong line.
They want the one, that will give them, more time.
To finish each task, and show the ones behind them,
When they get this far, in the line, they are at the right end."

I wake to smell
homemade bread.
All is well, I
Chose to wed
I wake to the wail
Of baby's voice.
My child is male,
He's God's choice.
I awake to thunder
And pouring rain.
A little more slumber,
God tends my grain.
I wake up old.
Soon life is done.
I carried my load,
And it was fun.

The Gift

If God said to you, "This gift I will give,
What part of your life would you rather not live?"

No reason to give up the first three years.
Most of us can't remember our diapers and tears.
The next three years, we can't wait to start,
School and movies, and getting real smart.

Grade school years, we thought would be great.
Some they shattered dreams, and taught them to hate.
Some got spoiled and vain and rude.
Some made up life, to suit their mood.
Some just drifted along with the crowd.
Others got tough, and mean, and loud.
Maybe, some eased back to see,
If there was something, yet to be.
Jr. and High school had to be best.
We jumped into them, with vigor and vest.
We were still young, and eager to learn.
Facing unrelenting obstacles at every turn.

The ones who hated with dreams no more,
Scorned and tricked, to even the score.
The vain and spoiled spent most of that time,
Demanding and pouting, pushing to the front of the line.
When you make up the world, the way you want it to be.
You're still at the bottom after climbing the tree.
All the way up, you only saw, what you wanted to see.
The ones who drifted, with no will of their own,
Were used by the rest, and then just left alone.
Some of the tough, mellowed out when they saw
Being mean and loud is a Devil's flaw.
And what about those, who eased back to wait?
Was riches, or happiness, or eternal peace, their fate?

These are the years, that patterned, the rest.
We can't give them up, or we wouldn't exist.

The next 30 or 40 years you have one, or two, or more mates.
Maybe have children, see the world, or just a few states.
Whatever you do, this is the main part.
If you give this up, no reason to even start.

The golden years are the end of the line.
If we survive, they should be the best time.
Some give them up through no fault of their own.
Some are hungry, some are sick, some left all alone.
Some oldies are content as they putter away,
Doing chores and facing problems that come with each day.
Some don't even know they grew old.
Some sit in darkness, seeing nothing unfold.
Some, can't hear the slightest sound.
Some are crippled, and can't get around.
Some had these problems from the day they were born.
You don't have to get old to feel tired and worn.

So God, this is one gift You don't have to give.
It's Your job, not mine, which parts I will live.

There Are a Few Things, God

There are a few things I want you to help me with, God,
That others inflict, that put my heart and mind in a
hopeless fog.

One, is when there is something I have rightfully earned,
It is given but demeaned and rebelled at every turn.

Then the times I give to one, and the other is angry or hurt,
I give with no malice, nor with feelings do I flirt.

When I feel great joy at a political event,
I arouse anger in a friend at the message I, or it sent.

I have to hold back any triumph I've gained, because
There is always someone who tries to make me feel ashamed.

A child in my care constantly rebels in a grumble.
I react with insanity and fail to be humble.

The times when a violent or immoral deed is acted out
By someone I trusted, beyond a shadow of a doubt.

Most of all, when I feel secure, the one I love, loves me too,
Says, "What makes you so sure my love is only for you?"

These are the few times, God, when only you can help.
I'll do my best with the rest of my life, myself.

My Grief

Don't interfere, my grief is my own.
With my way of grieving, leave me alone.

I don't want to be told how I must feel.
It's too confusing, when I'm trying to heal.

The relation to me is a private thing.
The comfort I need, only time will bring.

If you want to help with my earthly chores,
I'll welcome this gesture, with open doors.

Don't think I'm callous with a silent reply,
If you try to answer my feelings of why?

God, in His wisdom, will bring peace to me.
He alone knows why death had to be.

When I need to talk, I'll call on you.
I need only, your presence now to help me through.

Don't think for a minute I'm being unkind.
I know how you feel, and your state of mind.

You want very much to bring me relief.
Just knowing you care will help my grief.

Let just me, and the Lord, mend inside.
The road's built for two on this bumpy ride.

I'm So Sorry

I'll do this tomorrow, I'm too busy today.
You're always wanting to laugh and to play.

You won't leave me alone to get things done.
I can't ignore my work, and just have fun.

Little one, I'm so sorry as I kneel on your grave.
God gave me such beauty, then took it away.

He put you down here, for me to love.
But, I was too busy, so he returned you above.

BRAD HAYES

Teaching Faith

A tiny seed lay in a rugged worn hand.
Placed in a tiny hole, and covered with dirt, from the land.

Watered and weeded, with exceptional care.
It grew healthy and strong, preparing to bear.

The worn rugged hand, and alert watchful eyes,
Made sure nothing harmful, invaded the earth where it lie.

When the time came, the fruit, was perfectly ripe.
The grower and tender took the first bite.

He took the fruit, laid it in a small child's hand.
Then gently but firmly, so the child would understand,

He said, "This is just for you, and while you are near,
In the same way, I will tend you year after year.
So when the time comes, you must be on your own,
I will be content with what I have grown."

Into the rugged worn hand slipped the small chubby one.
As they went down the path, with the setting sun.

BOOM
BOOM
BOOM
LOUD
BRAD HAYES

Is It Quiet in Heaven?

In Heaven it's quiet. It's noisy on earth.
Must be why we yell, when we arrive at birth.

In Heaven we're told there is no sorrow or pain.
It doesn't snow, no wind, and it doesn't rain.

If we didn't know sorrow, we couldn't feel pleasure.
How can we enjoy some days if there is no change in the weather?

If you're always mellow, and you never sin,
If you never lose, then you never win.

If you never hate, then how do you love?
If there isn't a vulture, why have a dove?

How can you be good, if you've never been bad?
How can you feel peace, if you've never felt mad?

If no one is mean, how do we know if someone is kind?
If nothing is lost, then there is nothing to find.

If there is nothing to find, there's no reason to search.
Heaven won't have schools or libraries, or even a church.

In Heaven they say we won't need to be fed.
You'll never get tired, so you won't need a bed.

There won't be any colors, everything is white.
If there is no dark, how can there be light?

If when we get there, everyone is the same,
Why bother on earth to improve our brain?

And, if it's true, we'll come back someday,
Why even bother to go away?

A lot are conceived, but are never born.
Like creating a garment that is never worn.

Does the unborn have a soul, and where do they wait?
Do they get another chance to appear, and take shape?

And if we are born, but only live for awhile,
Was it preordained, did Heaven plan every mile?

If you grow old, you will look back and see,
Everything in your life was meant to be.

Every grief that you suffered, or joy that you knew,
Was meant to happen, and only to you.

You'll wish you were dead when your life is a mess.
But what's up in Heaven, is anyone's guess.

When our bodies are dead, can our spirits freely act?
Are our memories and knowledge still intact?

The greatest thing that would weigh on my mind,
If I knew I left someone who needed me behind.

And if we are recycled, like some people say,
Why does our population increase every day?

You better not worry about Heaven right now
Because it's never revealed until your final bow.

Then it's too late, if you don't like it there.
So just like living, dying's not fair.

If in Heaven our spirits and minds are freed.
Then Heaven is silent, cause words we won't need.

No questions, no answers, nothing to solve.
Well, maybe this earth's not so bad, after all.

The Knowledge of Birth

The world is round, no beginning, no end.
Where space goes, our minds can't comprehend.

Earthly objects change substance and shape, but go somewhere.
Seed, then plants, then mulch, then coal, diamonds, oil, or smoke in the air.

Plants and then seed, chicken then egg, then water, then steam.
Or was it the seed, the egg and vapor, first on the scene?

Whatever came first, God created and blessed.
But, where did God come from, and the substance and knowledge, he possessed?

God can communicate and teach with a thought.
We can think and wonder why, but how we know not.

Our perception is limited to a front and a back.
Or inside and outside, or bottom and top of a stack.

A circle doesn't begin or end, but it is surrounded, somehow
By air, or paper, or water, or dirt, or the past, future or now.

Space is forever, with nothing it will collide.
But even forever, like a circle, has to have another side.

Helen Keller was deaf and blind, but could smell, taste and feel.
By training her senses, life was revealed.

Different people, animals, bugs, fish, reptiles living species, everywhere.
Formed by, sperm, genes, molecules, grown with water, food, loving and air.

The moon, the sun, the stars, and no matter how far back you go,
God or Nature had to begin with something to make it all grow.

Man, by faith, can believe God planned and created all that we are.
Scientists can study and guess, but only with what's here, there isn't anymore.

So after four thousand years, and eons of time,
We only know what God has instilled in our minds.

And if you are searching for the formula to life and earth,
Don't waste any more time, God controls the knowledge of birth.

God loves me,
And not you.
What I say
Is very true.
I am a child,
Part of God.
I'm your master,
You are my dog.
This is the way
I learn to love.
You are my teacher
Sent from above.

Responsibility

Blame someone else when things go wrong,
Or the weather, or God, or any object, that comes along.

You never did anything to take the blame.
Your parents are responsible for your life and your name.

While you were little, you were learning the rules.
If you didn't learn anything, it's the fault of the schools.

Now, you're a teenager, and if you're not too dumb,
You'll not get caught, when you go out to have fun.

Well so far, you've managed to stay guilt free.
Maybe not your conscious, but what everyone else can see.

If you live the rest of your life blaming someone else
For everything that happens, or you do yourself.

You'll get obnoxious and proud and end up alone.
Love or consideration of others you've never shown.

You'll never have any rewards if you've never knelt to
pray,
To at least tell the Lord you did something wrong today.

Seasons to Come, The National Library of Poetry

What's Under the Snow?

Mommie, what's under the snow?
Your hat you lost, I needed to sew.

Daddy, what's under the snow?
The lawn that Daddy has to mow.

Grandpa, what's under the snow?
The stream where fishing I go.

Grandma, what's under the snow?
My pretty flowers in springtime grow.

Brother, what's under the snow?
My broken down car they need to tow.

Sister, what's under the snow?
My lipstick and brand new hair bow.

Uncle, what's under the snow?
My wallet I lost with all my dough.

Aunt, what's under the snow?
Oh, Sweetie Pie, Auntie don't know.

God, what's under the snow?
The Earth. It's asleep, waiting for spring to show.

The ground is resting, so there will be a good crop.
So be very careful when you play on top.

He's Not Dumb

A little boy doesn't want to believe
He can't control all he perceives.

You can tell him a fact he can't comprehend,
If you are a grown-up, not a mutual friend.

He will believe everything his teacher said,
Even if he didn't get it right in his head.

Once he realizes what you said is true,
He won't give in. The one wrong has to be you.

To save his pride you have to say,
"You are the one who told me yesterday."

His face lights up. You think he's the one
Who knows it all. He's not dumb.

Value

Value is real, it's not a dream.
It means highly regarded, with much esteem.

Where is a value planted to grow?
The perfect ground is in your soul.

The seed will form in another place.
A value seed is not to waste.

It can't be sold to satisfy greed.
It will not remain among villainous weeds.

The root of value was in the mind,
Of the first human being who appeared in time.

How the roots developed depended on the ward.
Value can stagnate if it is ignored.

When a value blooms, it's magnificent to behold.
Taught but not practiced, it will grow cold.
But value has the power to never grow old.

The most beautiful sight is value in bloom.
More intoxicating than the rarest perfume.

The seeds are planted by constant use,
To bloom again with kindness, caring, and truth.

I believe
The earth won't end.
It's meant to blend with the universe
For a perfect verse
With a steady flow,
Up and down it goes.
Our memories are stripped
On our mortal trip.
We have to be naive
When we enter and leave.
Nothing will make sense
Of earth's time spent.
It's combined in the plan
Of the lion and the lamb.
From the day we are born
Our soul will be torn,
Until we die,
With the question, "Why?"

A Crippling Guilt

There must come a time you have to let go,
Of a crippling guilt your mind is devoted to stow.

You cannot excel, or feel complete satisfaction,
When you've accomplished a deed, with quality action.

Your soul can be freed by accepting the blame.
Or forgetting and forgiving who caused your shame.

It's impossible to go back and erase your life.
You could be the only one who dwells on the strife.

Drift back through time, and sort it all out.
Don't take a detour on your backward route.

If there are any that you can work to amend,
Do it so they understand the message you send.

The rest forget, by confessing in your heart.
It's the only way for contentment to start.

I try not to wander so far from myself
That when I return, there is somebody else.
From the day I was born, I knew I was me.
No matter how much I change, there inside I will be.
If anyone else ever knows me that well,
I hope they will use discretion and never tell.

I Was Beckoned to Awake

I was beckoned to wake, there was much to do.
Instead of my room, I was somewhere new.
Maybe not new, but peaceful and mild
I had not seen so many who graciously smiled.
There was a mother holding a child to her breast.
She said, "My baby died, even though I did my best."
Years later, I closed my eyes to forget my physical pain.
I opened them because I heard my name.
There was my child, smiling so sweet.
"Mommy God said it was time that we meet."
Then ever so gentle the words, welcome home.
I'm always here to claim one of My Own.
I looked around to see all who were there.
I thought it would tell me, in life, how I fared.
I remembered the faces, but not the deeds,
I had completely forgotten what they believed.
God said, "You have finished your time on earth,
You had to know, the reason for birth.
If you hadn't achieved, or failed to learn,
I would have to prepare for you to return.
Your spirit is ready for another phase,
Your body returned to its earth grave.
The woman beside me asked, "May I speak?
If You part us now, my child will weep.
Will I have to leave my child behind?"
"She will go with you, you're both ready this time."
There is an eternal Hell, some people said,
Where all sinners go when they are dead.
That was a belief you were once told.
It's a Human way, for them to control.
Your Human form existed in a fog
Many proclaimed they knew the true God.
Hell is eternal. It's always around.
You pass through it, but you are not forever bound.

Every place you go requires a master,
So Satan rules over every disaster.
To stabilize chaos, there has to be rules,
They don't work without the right tools.
To make any sense of life's confusion,
Humans have to invent a working illusion.
How could you think I would rise on High,
And abandon Mine to weep and cry?
You just passed through Hell, and now I know
The next place your spirit is prepared to go.
I don't judge you while in your earth form,
I knew your whole life before you were born.
If you never were wrong, you could never be right,
Without the dark, there could not be light.
If you sat on the fence and never jumped in,
You avoided good, so you could avoid sin
You will be there forever, but that is your choice.
Once you make a decision, you will hear My voice.
Forever means there is no final chapter.
It's a waste of time, worrying about forever after
When Humans think, I'm only going to save a few,
Then they are judging, and that's only My right to do.
I want My keep to do the best they can,
I guide them through when they don't understand.
You remember the calm, you remember the storm.
Your soul grew weary at the constant alarm.
While on Earth, you were serving your time,
You could not be you if I controlled your mind.
All on your own, you accomplished your task.
I was always there, but I never asked,
For you to love and obey, or waste your time with fear.
I knew the things your spirit lacked before you left here.
Your trials were arranged, so when you came back,
Your spirit could continue on the right track.
God, I know what is sin and what is not, but nothing more.
That's all you required to pass through Heaven's door.
Now it is written for eternity,
You are exalted, I am proud of thee.

If you really believe what you hold inside,
Nothing can penetrate your bona fide hide.
When one you admire impertinently bestows
The cunning remark, "You are wrong you know,"
Because you are human, it hurts when it hits.
Then it falls to the ground in atmos bits.
It's got nothing to do with arithmetic,
It's the reality of faith that makes you tick.

When Mom Was Sober

You stand your ground, you are tough
You take care of yourself, when times are rough

Ain't nobody going to conquer you
Facing a challenge, you know what to do

You stand determined, never shed a tear
You would never reveal a hint of fear

The world's not kind, but what the heck
You can survive, any tangled wreck

You don't understand why you stand alone
You know you protect the place you call home

It's dirty and cold, barely enough food
Most of the time Mom's drunk and rude

It's been ten years since you were born
It's nothing new for most to scorn

Many times you've dodged a stone
In your direction, maliciously thrown

No one can penetrate your shield of protection
It's the only place you've not known rejection

Trying to remove you gets you real riled
Even though you are a scared, hungry child

You remember the love when Mom was sober
The pain won't come until you are much older

Dark is the night,
If you venture out.
A scary flight,
There is no doubt.
Everything can hide in the black screen.
All creatures collide with foe and fiend.
The darkness moans,
And never sleeps.
It must be the home
The devil's souls meet.

The Lawyer

I want to help you, but first I must know,
Did you do any deed to deserve this blow?

Did you do any harm that caused someone grief?
Are you a tyrant, a murderer, or a common thief?

You have to make sure you tell me the truth,
I'm not a cop, a judge, or a sleuth.

I'm a lawyer who wants to defend the right way.
If you are guilty, you do have to pay.

The reason why you committed this deed,
Is all the defense material, I need.

I will no longer use my position in life,
To set a guilty person free to again cause the same strife.

I'm going to turn over a new leaf,
And try to undo, some of the grief.

My profession has caused to the country I loved.
And to all the victims we've just pushed and shoved.

I have all the riches any human could want.
And the power to be able to snub and to flaunt.

A satin pillow for my head,
Then a small child looked up and said,
"Why did you help him when my Mommie is dead?"

When I was young,
I told my mind
What I sung
Would benefit mankind.
In my middle years
I was offered gold.
To praise and cheers,
My values I sold.
The end draws close
With foolish deeds
I can only boast
Of emptiness and greed.

I Can't Go On

Today I feel like I can't go on.
I feel like everything I do is wrong.

Maybe not wrong, but just no use.
My stabling control is hanging loose.

It's a point in my life I can't understand why
I can't just go to bed and forever lie.

I'm angry at each necessary chore.
That I do over and over just to face more.

It seems like the only thing, I get done
Is make life easier for some other one.

I know that sounds selfish and mean.
I can't do it all, too many on me lean.

I feel tired and guilty, and I want to rest,
Just peacefully float, above the river's crest.

But if I do that, I'll look back and see
The ones I love drowning because of me.

And that would be a lot worse to bear
Than quitting now because I've already done my share.

So, I guess I'll just take this day off.
Go out in the sunshine and play some golf.

When I feel bad today,
Tomorrow will start
Healing my mind and
Mending my heart
When it's physical pain
Through the night,
I feel much better
With the morning light.
If I can dream mental
Cares away,
Tomorrow will bring
A peaceful day.

Yesterday, Today, Tomorrow

Do you ever think, of what used to be,
Or wonder why now so much you never see?

Fifty years ago is so much more than yesterday.
Too many things have been lost, or buried away.

Things that were important no longer exist.
Like Sunday Dinner, and a walk, safe and brisk.

The Great Depression brought sharing to our door.
Pitching in and caring came with the second World War.

After that there was plenty if you worked honest and hard.
But after twenty years, the kids got bored.

They weren't taught the basics, or needed them to survive.
Social Security and Welfare kept the old and poor alive.

President Kennedy was killed in his prime.
A politician now will compare himself to that time.

If he's trying to impress the older generation,
He better look around, it's a whole other nation.

If you had some ambition, there were ways to excel.
Hippies and Viet Nam were when good values fell.

Rebellion and dodging was that era's worst strife.
Act and dress alike, no matter your status in life.

Most started wanting more than recognition and glory.
Greed and power became the main theme of thc story.

Grandpa and Grandma were no longer respected.
Raising kids without discipline got to be expected.

Music and movies got extremely obscene.
Real life got worse than our scariest dream.

Everyone stopped caring as long as you left them alone
Doors locked, mistrust, abuse, profanity, in every house and home.

Some could control and maintain some order.
Teaching by example got harder and harder.

I'm beginning to realize, restoration, won't work.
All the know-how's stuck in a deep dark murk.

And even if yesterday was claimed from its murky grave,
Too many are gone to know why it was saved.

Too much of the good stuff wasn't passed down.
If you're old enough to remember, just look around.

Time takes its toll, it never rests.
Everywhere, all the time bitter and sweet, are at their best.

Everyone enters and leaves at their own precise time.
What happened before, or what happens after, rarely enters their mind.

We only embrace the moment at hand.
Not much occurs exactly as planned.

If what worked yesterday was practiced today,
Maybe tomorrow would turn out in a different way.

There's no way to stop time from passing through.
Today became Tomorrow, and Yesterday too.

Today is gone, and Tomorrow is here.
Today slipped into another Yesterday, like the drop of a tear.

God Will Walk Me Home

Little one, isn't this a long distance from home?
Yes, but I'm not worried. God will walk me home.
What makes you think God has the time.
Because he likes me. He's a friend of mine.

He may be angry you wandered away.
He might be worried, but angry words He doesn't say.
If He is worried, won't you feel bad?
Oh Yes, I don't want to do anything to make Him sad.

I will go back right now, before He sees I am gone.
He might already know, you've been gone so long.
I will hurry back, and if He does know,
I'll ask Him to forgive me, and hold me close.

Do you think He will forgive and do what you ask?
Yes, if I have never lied to Him in the past.
God always knows if you are really sorry.
It's Mom and Dad, who might not believe my story.

ZZZZ
100 S.
27348
BRAD HAYES

The EPA said birds can't
Survive where traffic,
Smog, and the city thrive.
There is a sign that reads,
"Don't feed the pigeons,"
And a bargain sale board
Pecked to smidgens.
In the middle of a big
Highway cloverleaf,
A little bird on a stop
Light pole was fast asleep.
They moved him away from
His hotel and neon sign.
The forest was quiet and dark
All the time.
He finally found a familiar
Place to ease his mind.
People might be surprised
How well birds adjust,
And everything else
Without any fuss.

Color

I don't like you because, your skin is black.
I don't like you, any color your skin lacks.

Your skin is red or yellow, stay away from me.
You're brown, you're someone I don't want to see.

This is how it all began.
Color is why Man hated Man.

After hundreds of years things were getting set straight.
We were getting educated at a pretty good rate.

When it was obvious we could respect each other,
Again, some had to perpetrate a war with color.

Now, I hate you if you wear blue.
Or, the color red is why I hate you.

If the whole world was black or white,
Is that what it will take to stop this fight?

History has proven what color you are, or wore,
Is the reason the world will start a war.

It's not really the color, but it's a good excuse
To get even because someone suffered an abuse.

Side by side, color fights when the war begins.
Hate comes from inside, not the color of our skin.

It takes just a few to set the trap.
The reasons are different, but color takes the rap.

There is enough sunshine
For the universe.
We don't care or wonder
Which star was first.
We have some guidance
On our originate,
We can choose for destiny
Or the hand of fate.
We are only here for a breath of air
To improve and leave clean
To the future heir.
We don't need to dictate,
Just install some rules.
When we meet an entering spirit in the exchange space,
Whisper peace, you are armed with faith.

For Pity's Sake

When I waller in pity, it has to be.
I can blame others for the deeds of me.

It's not my fault, I'm feeling so low.
Others have caused, my tears to flow.

When others need a target, I am it.
They shoo me away with careless wit.

I know they haven't treated me fair.
They are not even sorry, as I flagrantly stare.

I'll show them, I'll work like a dog,
I'll plow my way through this demeaning fog.

When I'm done, everything will shine,
And I will have subdued my inflicted whine.

I know when my house is dirty, and I am procrastinating,
Some one around me will respond to debating.

I can force out, a negative "WHY?"
That can get me going with a cruel reply.

My integrity's been wounded, so I'll show them.
Once more, I've been inspired, by pity again.

Suicidal

Have you ever had mental pain so bad,
That physical pain is what you wish you had.

When the torment inside has finally won,
You're not even afraid of a bullet from a gun.

The mental infliction may or may not be your fault.
You may or may not be able to call a halt.

If you have done something you just can't face,
Injury or death can draw attention away to their place.

Somethings in life, cannot be undone.
Your mind is one part that cannot run.

When you tell another you need to tell the whole story.
If you do die by your hand, lies will take the glory.

The way back to healing is a confusing appeal.
Truth is the right medicine for you to heal.

If you cannot regain a love that is lost,
Or obtain perfection because of the cost.

Those are the things you must accept and share.
Your body is fragile, but your soul can be repaired.

A Raging Guilt

Whose emotions are in need of repair?
I can't sort it out, and that isn't fair.
My thoughts are trapped by a raging guilt.
When I get the three gold bars the machine says,
"Tilt."
What I do is normal to me, but always wrong.
My confiner says stop, or you won't belong.
The pain can be quenched with a handful of pills,
But the burial hole, only I will fill.
It lurks in the dark for the time I will
"Slip."
Where I can insanely thrash to be free of death's
"Grip."
Constantly, constantly, I can't decide,
If life or death is where I will abide.

A Muse to Follow, The National Library of Poetry

Heavenly Words

I never liked the word forgive,
You always do something wrong as you live.

But then I don't like the word wrong.
It's a matter of opinion as you go along.

Speaking of opinion, who really knows,
If a deed needs repenting because it caused woe?

You must repent, some will say,
You need to be forgiven for your deed today.

Now, wait a minute, it wasn't you I upset.
You think I'm wrong because of what someone else said.

In my opinion, I have the right, you see,
To make my own decisions, about me.

Wrong, right, forgive, the word repent,
I heard them forever, wherever I went.

I will repent, if in God's opinion I should.
If anyone knows if I'm wrong or right, God would.

No human being should ever be so smug,
To think they have the power to forgive or judge.

My Attitude

Grow up Maurine, you're too old to care
And should know by now life isn't fair.
You want too much of human emotion,
Kindness, acceptance, and steadfast devotion.
What do you want? You have more than most.
Accept criticism and never boast.
When other people cause you pain,
And you rebel with actions that are the same,
It doesn't work, it degrades your soul.
On and on, bitterness takes its toll.
After all these years, you've never undone
A single opinion of anyone.
I guess some are right about my attitude,
But I'll never believe I deserve the rude.
I honestly respect another's view.
Unworthy actions I have the right to refuse.
And if an attitude is what it takes,
I'll keep it in tact to weed out the fakes.

The Rumor

A lot of people I know are my friends
A lot of people are apt to pretend.

Under the pretense of caring for you,
They undermine actions others do.

I love to see the look on their face,
When they fail to achieve an erroneous disgrace.

I heard someone say, "You are old and fat."
"That's strange, I thought, I was the one, who said that."

Oh well, if another wants to take the credit,
I won't waste my time to fret it.

Next time I have an opinion of myself,
I just won't tell anyone else.

Then when a rumor gets back to me,
I won't feel betrayed by my friend or the one who
pretends to be.

You can totally control another with guilt,
Identify and push their button marked wilt.
The wires are connected to many or one.
Installed for reasons they may or may not have done.
Someone in their life invented and put to action
A device that could drive them to total distraction.
The gears start to turn when they hear mistrust,
And will turn forever because they never rust.

Words of Destruction

Sticks and stones, will break my bones, but names will
never hurt me.
You know that's not true, your words in my heart will
ever be.

When you call me a slurry, profane name, it will always
fester inside.
I'm a human being, you might not notice, but I have
pride.

Do you ever say, excuse me, I'm going to break your bone?
No, your weapon is rude words, in a demeaning tone.
You take the easy way out, consideration and fairness,
you've never known.

Insults and slurs must give you satisfaction.
You can take a bow for the best attraction,
To see a prejudice fool in uncontrolled action.

One day, when you are wondering why you are hated,
It's the harmful environment your words created.

When you open your mouth to utter destruction,
First, educate your mind with humanity instruction.

Peel appearances from the outside,
You can't tell us apart looking at the inside.

Unless it's written all over our heart,
Words spoken and received deformed the main part.

If beyond a doubt, there is positive proof
That someone has acted insanely uncouth,
Thinking the only way to rule the world,
Into violent possession they blatantly hurled.
Somehow we were betrayed because we were sad.
We would accept anything just to feel glad.
You know you shouldn't, but you look away.
You shut out reality of what they say.
You'll embrace the part that lifts you up.
You are tired of emptiness and want a full cup.
It doesn't matter if it is filled with deceit,
It warms your belly and lets you sleep.
As you close your eyes, the reaper waits,
One last moment of peace before you enter Hell's gates.

Windows of the Soul, The International Society of Poets

Being a Good Fireman

I want to be a fireman when I grow up,
So does my sister, if she can keep her mouth shut.

I can't believe it, she's not uttering a sound.
She must be serious, she's firehouse bound.

I told her she has to be very brave,
There will be a lot of people she'll have to save.

You have to fold the hose, and climb the ladder.
Crawl through windows, so you can't get fatter.

Cook your own meals, and do the dishes.
Wait on the Chief, whatever he wishes.

If you ever get to drive the truck,
And it scares you, you can't throw up.

You probably will have to shave your head.
If you breathe in smoke, it will make you shed.

You'll have to shower with all the guys
So she better get over being shy.

Being a Donkey is the first rank you hold.
Then a Horses Ass, when you get old.

You will get bow legged from sliding down the pole.
Doing the paper work is the firegirl's role.

Girls have to train at least ten years.
Protect the fire hydrant, so dogs don't get near.

If a Fireman gets sick and starts to droop,
You have to make him chicken soup.

Make all the beds every morning.
She said, "I think I'll get married, it won't be as boring."

I changed her mind without getting rough.
Mom said, "Who will do all that stuff?"

In the line of duty, it has to be done,
Being a good fireman isn't all fun.

A Child's Sweet Breath

There's a cruel awakening, held in reserve,
That no mortal human, could ever deserve.

A few have been dealt this heart breaking sight.
Leaving flashes of pain for the rest of their life.

A person can try to describe the grief,
But its effect on the mind is beyond belief.

Forever regrets, there wasn't time,
To prevent this injustice to human kind.

You always wonder, did I really try?
I just don't know, is your minds reply.

If you only could find something that made sense,
How can you fight when there is no defense?

You're pleasant and kind to all you meet.
Always deep inside, you silently weep.

After the first time viewing such harm,
You prepare for the worst at the sound of the alarm.

If it's declared those present will burn,
Then prepare my heart, and help me learn.

It was a general incident that caused this result.
It's too much to bear, thinking it's my fault.

Please God, this time let there be no death,
I can douse the fire, and when life is left,
I will know content, feeling, a child's sweet breath.

I wrote this poem for a fireman who could not get to three children before they were burned to death.

A Conscious Guide

When you are little, someone falls, you laugh
Or slips under the water while taking a bath

It's an instinct instilled in your soul
Of your mind, it will always control

That caused a need for a conscious and will
The conscious to be developed because of the instinct instilled

Control of actions is the hardest part
You will always laugh, but learn to cry in your heart

When you get older, all the time you are assisting
You are concerned, but a smile you are resisting

You have sinned in your heart because of your thoughts
STOP believing that, it's only what you have been taught

Your mind is automatic, it's your actions that count
With caring teachers, your goodwill starts to mount

Don't worry about what pops in your mind
It's God's way of giving you a conscious guideline

Once you have mastered, everything, on the list
The instinct thought is controlled and you won't proceed amiss

Do we love most of all
Our season of birth?
Is it then we feel closer
To the knowledge of our worth?
The first three months of every new year
Is the time for poets, warmth,
Drinking and cheer.
The next three months
The babies of spring.
They love flowers, warm breezes,
And learn how to sing.
Summer's three months when
The world lives and dies.
Its offspring loves fun,
Starry nights and contented sighs.
Three final months, if
You are born in the fall,
You harvest and enjoy
The labors of all.

A Disguise Is Worn

Long ago, a world was formed
For spirits to exist, where a disguise is worn

Others will view all the disguises and wonder
Only the adorned will know what is under

Words will be spoken by most of them
But it's only a guess if it's real or a whim

Some will think the eyes reveal
They are part of the disguise you cannot seal

If that is true, then the blind are complete
Their disguise is the ultimate illusion feat

It's easy if you detect vibrations of the voice
Silence keeps the secret, by God's or your choice

A frown or a smile is all that it will take
But those two expressions, the disguise can fake

Some are exploited, or intimidated by a tear
Three reasons to cry, pain, joy and fear

Also a tear can be dutifully forced
When the disguise wants to set its own course

All those senses draw away from the main part
The disguise is a master at shadowing the heart

But then, this disguise, works both ways
Your spirit can't see through the skin's haze

On the inside of the spirit's disguise
Is total darkness when the disguise closes its eyes

In spite of the darkness, the spirit has thoughts
Of what it saw, heard or felt, or keenly caught

So now the dilemma starts to unfold
The disguise was so clever to think it controlled

What a wonderful plot God has achieved
When the inside and out start to agree

When the disguise is old, and getting thread bare
The spirit will then be prepared

To go back to the place before it was born
Where it can excel because no disguise is worn

If God Doesn't Care

If God doesn't care, why should I?
First, we have to know what catches God's eye
Does he notice both, a little fib and a great big lie?

Just a little dirt swept under the rug
Can you kill a black widow, and a lady bug?
Can you go "All the way" or stop at a friendly hug?

A couple of pennies, no one will miss
Pick one or two roses, or all the irises
Love all the children, or just one gets a kiss

You won't eat one that is blemished from a bowl of fruit
You throw away the ugly and keep only the cute
Imperfection bores you, so you ignore the blind and the mute

You pamper whatever suits your mood
To the rest you indulge in being rude
The only intake you require is your food

I've already wasted too much of my time
Jotting down the assessment of your feeble mind
A dime a dozen can buy all of your kind

If you walk away and do not do your share
Because you feel your part isn't fair
It doesn't bother me, so why should God care?

Go ahead, run away
You don't like
Anything I say.
Take these earplugs
And when some thug
Talks to you rude,
You won't come
Unglued.

It's My Problem to Fix

My opinion is no reflection on you,
My heart is yours, but not my mind too.

We are one in the sense of love,
And all the instructions, from God above.

But the daily news, and what's written in books,
What I eat, what I like, or the way I look,

Is mine alone, and I want you to respect that.
You love your dog, I love my cat.

If your dog is hungry, I will feed him.
If he chews up my slipper, he'll get a smack on his chin.

If my cat gets lonely and cuddles on my lap,
You stop swatting her off with the brim of your hat.

I'm going to be wrong, a whole lot of the time.
You don't have to punish me that decision is mine.

Have faith that I know what I'm talking about
Or at least the right to express without constant doubt.

There are plenty of things you do I don't like,
But after thirty years, I've never gone on strike.

Please don't keep telling me to do what I'm told.
The dynamite's wick is almost gone, I'll soon explode.

And all of the thoughts I've kept inside,
Will be the fuel for my leaving ride.

Then when I goof, or it seems that I do,
It's my problem to fix and doesn't concern you.

In My Room, For Annie

Annie Lived in Port Orange, Florida

Four foot, eight inches tall, fourteen years old
At death, twenty-eight pounds, curled up in a fetal fold.
Cerebral palsy took some sight, some sound
And retarded some thoughts while she was mortal bound
For three months she was confined on a floor mat
Not fed, not loved, only two knew where she was at
What did they say when they reported her death?
"She didn't wave this morning, she had no more breath."

Another Annie in Europe fifty years back
Was also confined to her room by a heinous act
The past Annie put her pain into words
Please God, tell me the one now you heard
Lying alone, were you holding her hand?
Could her eyes see visions of another land?
Did she walk in a field of cool green grass?
Did she giggle and sing with Annie of the past?
A birthday cake with fourteen candles that danced and glowed
Ribbons in their hair that playfully flowed

Poor little Annie, she was never touched or held
She had no control of her functions and she smelled

Don't cry little Annie, it's not you and me who failed
At Buchenwald, the odor of my kins' flesh was inhaled
Like me, you are hated because you don't fit
In a place that fatuity has control of it
I know you love music and I do too
The words of the songs are speaking up for me and you
Many are now gathered to hear our prayer
They know how we feel, they really care
So never again can the tyrants resume
The actions of evil that sentence us to doom
And we won't cry when we hear "In My Room"

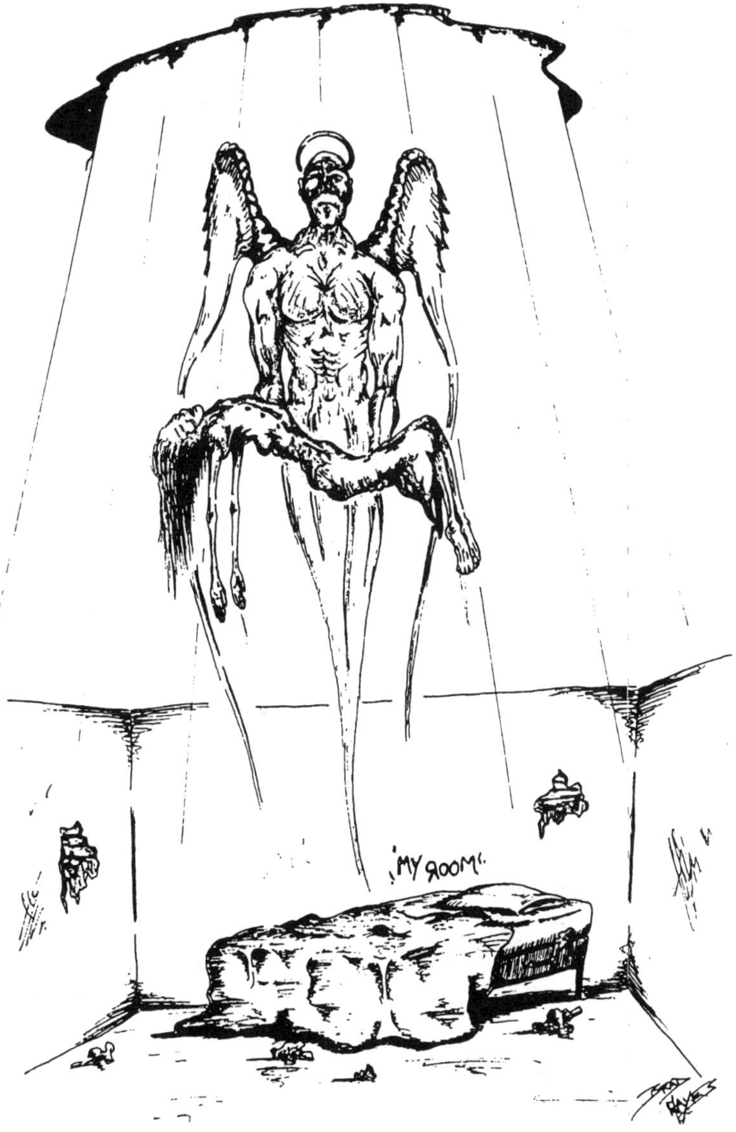
MY ROOM

BRAD HAYES

The Old Dirt Road

I remember so well an old dirt road.
That warmed my feet, no matter how cold.

I liked to sit down and push the dirt in a pile.
Or draw a round face with a great big smile.

I'd pick the dirt up in the palms of my hands.
Through my fingers would fall the part that was sand.

In the early morning, the dirt road was cool.
Always blackened my socks on my way to school.

Way down the road came a big cloud of dust.
That would change directions with every wind gust.

It seemed like forever before I could see
If someone was coming, to visit me.

More often than not the vehicle flew right on by,
With the wave of a hankie or a masculine cry.

Seemed only a blink before it was gone
And the dirt settled down where it belonged.

When I was young, the dirt road didn't end.
Every few miles lived a relative, or friend.

In the fall it was covered with acorns and leaves.
And weeds and grass, and flowers that made me sneeze.

The winter winds blew the dirt into whirls,
Lifted acorns from the reach of scampering squirrels.

The snow fell real soft, turned everything white.
Till a few tire tracks threw the dirt back into sight.

Everything froze and the road had three tracks.
Except for the slide ruts and the drifting snow packs.

Spring was the villain that started the thaw.
Your boots stuck so often, your feet would get raw.

Pushing someone stuck, you would get a mud bath.
When they were free, you would wave good-bye and laugh.

Sometimes, you would run, and jump in to ride.
They couldn't stop as they slid, side to side.

The road would dry hard, with ruts up and down.
It was rough and bumpy on the trip into town.

Summer would come and the road smoothed its shape.
You would head on down, bare feet, fishing pole and bait.

The dirt road is gone, and there in its place,
A big super highway, built for a high speed race.

We are suppose to be thankful for progress, we're told.
Well, I'm thankful I've memories of The Old Dirt Road.

I used to love every
Drop of rain.
Now there's too much, too often,
It's not the same.
How wonderful every flake of snow.
Now it's driven by the winds
That furiously blow.
And the sun felt good,
Dry and warm.
Stay out of it now, it causes
Great harm.
Each season brought the gift
Of a welcome toy,
The weather, like the world,
has left little to enjoy.

Him

If there wasn't a God, who could you blame,
For accidents and death that can't be explained?

There is the Devil, but he's only a tool
That can prod you to the actions of a fool.

If you don't believe in God, then Satan you don't need.
It's only fate that caused you to act, unmindful to heed.

Human words and actions, breed disgrace.
You wouldn't judge if you weren't trying to take God's place.

There are some mouths that are like a gun,
So many are injured when the mouth cocks to run.

When you are in peril and there's no place to flee,
You state, "Oh God, why did You let this happen to me?"

You want something so much, your thoughts run amuck.
When not delivered, it's God's fault you have bad luck.

Untimely death of a loved one, what do you say?
"I don't understand, God, why You took them away."

Maybe you never had any of those thoughts.
You accept the blame, or shame, or fate, and pay the cost.

It's still a lot easier to get through life,
If you can blame God for most of the strife.

When it gets to the point, you just can't win.
There is nobody left to blame, but Him.

I watch the news, or get stirred by a review,
The thought is there right out of the blue.
Some invisible force puts a pen in my hand.
The words are composed as only God can.
All of my words from God I borrow,
What I write today, I can't remember tomorrow.
I'm very content at what the world sees.
God did a good job unscrambling me.

Walk Through Paradise, The International Society of Poets

What's the Matter?

I want to be patient, and very kind,
But others are driving me out of my mind.

We preach and we watch things done the wrong way,
Harshness then regret performed every day.

Why do I have to resort to threats of grief
For peace and quiet, and worry relief?

You hate yourself for not being a saint
When you have to enforce or endure a complaint.

Just when you've learned to live with yourself,
You find out that fact bothers somebody else.

Stop worrying about it, I've often been told.
So I stop and the whole world gets out of control.

Then I have to start over to get things in order
I've only accomplished to make life harder.

Maybe things aren't as bad as they seem,
But I can't sort them out, if you know what I mean.

I'm very good at saying what you should do,
But when it's my problem, I haven't a clue.

The Human Mind

I don't understand the Human Mind,
Even if, the mind is mine.

I know everyday the things I should do,
But my mind keeps changing, all day through.

Unforeseen events will alter the day,
So some planned things I can't do anyway.

My mind's forever sorting challenges I meet,
There is no escape because I dream when I sleep.

But it isn't my mind that needs any rest,
My soul and body are the guilty pests.

My mind's never tired, it does get confused
It will keep on working, as long as it's used.

And I will exist forever in time.
The earth claims my body, God claims my mind.

Change the Subject

It's not fair that I can't cope,
And a willful child causes loss of hope.

I can resolve the problem when there is only one.
Disagreements between two, I just want to run.

When they are good I feel peace and pride.
When they are bad, I wither inside.

The contented times I completely forget
Were they just a dream my mind beget?

The feeling that chaos will never end
Is what whimpering and fighting children send.

I lose control and desperately shout.
This sends them into an insoluble pout.

With this I say, "I don't care what you do."
The reply is always, "You don't love me like I love you."

First it's rebellion, then a doggie love lick.
The only way out is to change the subject.

Child, You Are Wrong!

Child you are wrong, I've told you before,
Why do you insist, it makes me so sore.
When I get mad, you are definitely in danger.
When I start into action, I'll seem like a stranger.

There won't be any kindness on my sweet smiling face.
You will no longer be treated with Amazing Grace.
The fireworks will start, I'll forget your name.
On my sympathy, you will have no claim.

You better go out and purchase some armor.
After I'm through, I won't be a mourner.
It'll be the greatest satisfaction I've ever known.
I'll wave a victory flag wherever I roam.

If you ever again say, "I KNOW IT ALL."
You better prepare for your worst downfall.
I was seeking my fortune when I was your age.
You pout and demand, then explode with rage.

You think you've mastered the perfect indignant show.
When I preform, the whole world will know
You are still a child, and not what you seem,
Dress like a lady, talk like a saint,
YOU ARE ONLY THIRTEEN!

The Land of Opportunity

I was born into the land of opportunity
An American with the right to be equal and free

Raised to be proud of who I am
Thankful my home is American Land

Always looked at the leaders and teachers with awe
No one was finer, more respected, than the law

You could tell the good or the bad apart, Any place
They were betrayed by actions, and never their race

We cried and laughed at every picture show
No profanity, no sex, no exposure to violence uncontrolled

We were scared of shadows in the dark
Or stories we were told of a man eating shark

We were taught to work hard, and earn what we got
And to share what we had with those who had not

We did not turn our backs on violence or abuse
We learned control, and insanity was no excuse

I still remember how I was raised
If you broke the law, you did not get praised

One generation has come and gone
The next one will leave before very long

I watch my grandchildren with tears in my eyes
Soon there will be no one to hear their cries
I don't know how to teach them to survive

A Horse of Course

If you've never failed,
You've never won.
You didn't try, trying
Was the ultimate right
America supplied.
America excelled with
Choice, not force,
Unless you were a
Dictator, tyrant, or
"A Horse of Course"

Prison Rights

I murdered someone, I'm doing my time
It's punishment enough to be confined.
I'm very religious, it's not at all fair,
The prison rules, I have to cut my hair.

Why do you think you have any rights
After you robbed another of life?
You say it's inhumane to deface and violate,
Anything against the religion of the inmate.

I'll lose my dignity, my soul, there is nothing left.
I might as well join my victim in the jaws of death.
It's all right to rob, rape, and murder someone,
But my God will refuse me if my hair is not long.

I'm sure God won't notice if you are doing his will.
He's too busy receiving the victims you kill.

Who Is That Guy?

They are trying again to get God back in school.
They might even bring back THE GOLDEN RULE.

God doesn't like weapons or violence, we can't even swear.
You can't imagine how peaceful it will be if He is there.

It's hard enough to corrupt the kids who have Him at home.
They got to leave Him there and come here alone.

If we try to bring a gun, or sell some drugs,
He would be giving away, Education and Hugs.
Almost all the kids don't have any respect,
And now being polite, they totally reject.

We better watch out, if God gets His Way,
Some kids might think twice if they get to pray

WHO IS THIS GUY you are talking about?
I never knew anyone, who had that much clout.

Yeah kid, when you got to school, God wasn't here,
If you don't know Him at home, we can control you with fear.

If God's in your heart, from the day you are born,
It would be a lot harder to get you to harm.

All our weapons and violence are no match for
HIS MIGHTY SWORD.
If He gets back in, the teachers and parents will be
saying, "THANK THE LORD!"

WELCOME GOD!
SCHOOL
17
213CK

Fire Line

There is a fast-moving flame in the under brush,
With continuous fuel to feed its oncoming rush.

It scorches or engulf's everything in its path,
Leaving only the proof prepared that can survive its wrath.

When it gets to the trees, it will rise and crown,
Explode and claim more territory for miles around.

What will we do to halt its path to the trees?
Build a shelter for wind and discourage the slightest breeze?

This will slow it down, but it will smolder and creep.
It will be content to rest, but it and us will not sleep.

There is a way that has worked most of the time.
You have to design and construct a perfect fire line.

Someone supplies the tools, then all must participate,
Build it swift and right, so the resting flame will never wake.

Totally remove all fuel from its reach,
Back burn all bridges and trails it could breach.

Clear very deep, very wide, all trash to the fire's side.
When it has devoured its own, it will wither and die.

On the other side, the trees will prosper and grow unless
A hot ember was ignored, waiting to fly when the wind
again blows.

The ember can jump across the fire line to be nourished,
And continue once more to the point where it flourished.

So be ever vigilant with the ashes and the fire line.
Keep the ashes cold, the line deep and wide all the time.

While you are learning to quench and contain the fire,
Use the same method with life because evil will never tire.

The Glory Train

I wonder what in life I've yet to find.
Could it be a little or a lot, depends on my demise time.

I'm sort of hoping there is a lot in store.
I'm not near wise enough to go through Heaven's door.

I remember way back when I knew it all,
Because of my ego, I heard a distant call.

Why should you linger where there is no purpose?
Whatever else you obtain will just be surplus.

You know that surplus got used up real fast.
After sorting and wasting, the rest didn't last.

Now I know, while in this life's phase,
I have to stop living for constant praise.

There was always someone who knew more than me.
Once I accepted that fact, my pride set me free.

Now I can romp through the fields of life.
It doesn't matter if I win when I throw the dice.

Just to feel the joy of entering the game
Is the fare you need to board the glory train.

That's Not Fair

If you never felt,
"That's not fair."
Everyone would do, or more, than their share.
We wouldn't be better,
We wouldn't need praise.
We wouldn't feel cheated,
In a pouting haze.
If we never felt,
"That's not fair,"
We might become passive,
And cease to care, and
"That's not fair."

Whose Will Is It?

Life's always been hard, but not this strange.
Pa was out on the range, Ma was in at the range.

Pa's job was to plow and raise the food.
Ma's job was to cook and raise the brood.

It's kind of mixed up now as to who does what.
On most of the old ways, the door has been shut.

In one way it's sad, in another it's not.
Modern material, but old values should be taught.

A new kitchen range with home made apple pie,
Store bought clothes, modest and appealing to the eye.

The books on the shelves were *Little Women* and Mark Twain.
Now, sue your parents, they're the ones to blame.

The evening sounds, a cooing dove and a thank you prayer.
You could still hear them both, if enough people cared.

It's real nice to have roads that are paved.
But, it's easier for a speedy trip from birth to the grave.

Almost everyone is in love with the picture show.
I just wish they would stop adding what we don't need to know.

For love and marriage, there have always been, different
reasons,
And God knows with some mates, there is just no pleasing.

Nobody tries, to get along.
It's too easy to leave than try to belong.

A hospital saved many a life.
At home, babies died and sometimes the wife.

But if at home the babies were born,
It seemed a closer union was formed.

When you crossed the ocean, you sailed on a ship,
Now, the big, fast jets make it a quick trip.

Good or bad, time never stands still,
I wonder if the changes are God's or man's will?

I'm Not Going to Worry Anymore

I'm not going to worry anymore.
It doesn't do anything to even the score.

There is still more wrong than what is right.
Worrying doesn't stop the spreading blight.

When I try to enforce a preventive measure,
I'm told I'm a fool and nobody's saviour.

If it seemed to me my tactic worked,
It's got nothing to do with you, most reply with a smirk.

So what do I do with the rest of my life
When I can't make a dent in daily strife.

All of the wisdom I thought I had learned,
Isn't wanted by any demeaned and returned.

Have I acted that way to others I knew?
Did I forget to be kind, and demanded with words that were cruel.

If I did, I'm sorry, it wasn't on purpose.
What I felt inside was different than on the surface.

Every Second of Life

The child can't wait for a birthday to be,
The rest of the year they live, but don't see.

The weeks before Christmas are painfully long.
Thank God for shopping, preparing, and song.

Year after year, it's always the rule, the child
Can't wait for the beginning and the end of school.

Then there are seasons for one special day.
One event in the future wastes many a yesterday.

To reach the point in life when each moment is lived,
Is truly unselfish, we now give others the pleasures to
give.

We must set aside our eagerness for a future date,
So we don't miss one smile or sigh while we wait.

Life isn't the special awarding times. They will pass.
It's the preparing, the planting, and mowing the grass.

The Other's Not Perfect

In the beginning, you might, have a hint,
A broken promise, under the bed, a little lint.

It's kind of a relief, the other's not perfect,
What little that's wrong can be brought into check.

There are ups and downs, but nothing too bad.
It's better than anything in the past you had.

Then the broken promise becomes a constant lie.
The lint under the bed is six inches high.

If you keep your promise, I'll clean the dirt.
There's not enough laughter, and too much hurt.

The beginning is the message you sometimes send,
But most of the time, you're acting like the end.

When the bonding begins, you have this faith
That forever is sealed without a turbulent wait.
The storm clouds gather, but you don't prepare.
You depend on the other to do their share.
The journey gets flooded with careless mistakes.
The seal starts to crack, and soon will break.
When we don't remember the seal was burned with trust,
Then the full fledged storm will cause the seal to bust.

Finally Forsaken?

Just like I got here, I'm walking back home.
Only this time, I'll be walking alone.

From there to here, I've carried the whole load.
I never complained, just did, what I was told.

And it didn't do me one bit of good.
You still aren't there, even when you could.

I tried to hold you with my good deeds.
Instead of tending to your sluffing needs.

It's going to be boring to have no one to save.
I won't forget you, I'll mow the grass on your grave.

Preparation

I've turned to stone, smooth and hard,
I can't even appreciate an award.

I wish for death, but not for me.
It's for the one who will pay my fee.

It's what I owe for life's abuse.
I piled up the debt with a feeble excuse.

I got tired of toil, and spent for fun,
I know the blame lies with no other one.

The streams of life have managed to smooth,
But hardened my heart for the desire to improve.

I can't stop the thought I harbor each day,
That the one who frowns will go away.

Stolen was my dignity I had managed to save,
Death will cancel the debt, and take it to the grave.

But I often wonder when only bitterness is left,
If it's God's way of preparing me for death.

Not What You Seem

You are not what you seem, if the truth be told.
You appear the strongest when you lost control.
When all around is confused and pushed to grieve,
You shrug with disgust, then turn and leave.
I felt so denied, some guilt, but defiant.
You made me believe the lie, I wasn't reliant.
You could shout me down, make me dodge and whine,
Till your body grew weak with the hands of time.
It gives me no pleasure, only sorrow to bear,
And regret as you die, never learning to share.

The Coy Game

Why do I cry myself to sleep?
You wouldn't know if you didn't peek.
You said, you didn't care if I cried all night.
Yet you mention my red eyes in the morning light.
You tell me to get used to being alone.
Then you call all day when I'm at home.
You keep telling me I have to let go.
Then you hold my hand, when I'm feeling low.
Are you playing a game, just seem to be sincere?
You say it's over, but the reason's not clear.
Existing in limbo, with all this confusion
Has helped me to reach a final conclusion.
I'll lock the door if you try to come back.
Leave nothing behind, I'll help you pack.
It brings pleasure to you to turn me away.
Your ego and fraud get bigger each day.
You will no longer see even one little tear,
There could be a million, but you won't be here.

Unknown User

Out of you and me, who is the abuser?
Which one of us claims the title, the user?

One of us is a manipulator.
Maybe it's both, but one, is greater.

I think it's you who is playing the game.
But I wonder sometimes if you feel the same.

Some things I do are wrong to you.
The reasons I did them, you haven't a clue.

But then confusion has worked both ways.
We both did good deeds without one word of praise.

We've gone on for years, not knowing each other,
Till we both feel we will hopelessly smother.

I've never known if I'm right or wrong, or
Which one of us to the other doesn't belong.

When we first met, you were all I wanted,
Ghosts of the past keep our life always haunted.

There is an invisible veil we can't penetrate.
I do know its lifting will come too late.

I've known death,
I didn't understand.
I've known death,
I've held the survivor's hand.
I've known death,
I've felt it wasn't fair.
I've known death,
I really didn't care.
I've known death,
Where I felt relief.
I've yet to know death
Where I was engulfed
With grief.

The Experienced Pathfinders

As they walk through life, they often bend,
Sometimes under the load, sometimes
To help a friend.
Some days their path leads them nowhere,
But the path is wide and they are
Willing to share.
They can walk alone, and carry the weight,
And they always take time to repair
A broken gate.
As they go down the path, they chart a map,
So others that walk there will know
Where they are at.
At the top of the map they write "Beware."
As a reminder, make sure your map is
A genuine pathfinder.

The Foolish Star

A very young star was winking one night.
It captured an audience way below its sight.

It was above, its subjects below.
It had to reach them with a captive show.

How could it span the great distance in space,
So the earth would always recognize this star's face?

There was also the moon it had to outshine.
It wanted to be able to say, the universe is mine.

The star figured out if it turned on the charm,
It would be applauded and adored by all who were born.

It got carried away with its last encore.
It's final, awesome sight was a falling star.

All through time, the greatest of all
Was not missed till its downfall.

Then it was forgotten and lost in space
Because another upcoming star took its place.

The Children of Now

Why do the ones who were not even born
Protest to a war that kept them from future harm?

They were born into peace and grew up free,
No future or past, only now they can see.

They are whining over rumors, and trying to undo
The method and reason, justice rose anew.

Makes you want to pound some sense into their heads.
They are sheltered and pampered, and over fed.

The children of now can't even imagine what might have been,
And how close the enemy came to a win.

They could never know how foolish they are,
Unless they succeed in starting another war.

They live in America that sanctions human rights.
They plot to destroy the common sense fight.

I want to tell them where their fiction comes from—
Drugs, alcohol, organized crime, gangs, fascism, the
losers, and the citizens who keep mum.

The path was paved with the loyal and the brave.
Right or wrong, they endured or went to their grave.

Not many now step forward to take a stand,
Because when they do, they're wrongfully damned.

The only reason God holds back His Wrath,
There still are a few, marked, the sacrifice calf.

A Racial Stage

Why is it some will pick a race
To nihilism or pile on degrading disgrace?

I've been guilty of silence and going along
With laughing and joking when I knew it was wrong.

Because of color, none has bothered me,
So why do I smugly and readily agree.

A period in history seemed to end,
Only to rise and repeat, again and again.

Why do some say, "I'm better than most,"
And continue the charade with Satan as their host?

The ones like me who know prejudice should cease,
Won't rebel or complain when invited to the feast.

Because we are afraid, or just don't care,
We have problems of our own we have to bear.

We join the foolish, or we stay out of reach.
We shut out or avoid the peace makers who preach.

I know I am guilty of an indignant whine,
When expected to solve a problem that is not mine.

I've been pushed to tears and prodded to rage,
But never had to perform on a racial stage.

Racism might end if we would all fight for the cause,
But if it does, only a few deserve the applause.

The dependent, the workers, the teachers, the law
Keep trying, but they are backed to the wall.
Disguised as their own, the devious rules,
And successfully portrays the common people as fools.

Shattered Hope

I hope this poem every cowboy will memorize.
Down around Amarillo I heard something that brought tears to my eyes.
I always admired a cowboy, but I felt let down.
I went into a store on the outskirts of town.
Gangs and graffiti were everywhere.
A few years ago there were only cowboys there.
I said I was surprised the cowboys hadn't wiped the gangs out.
She didn't seem to know, for a minute, what I was talking about.
Then she said, "A cowboy just turns and runs.
Cowboys no longer have any guns."
I said, "Not real guns. I mean courage, guts, and clout."
She said, "That is what I'm talking about."
My heart sank right down to a bottomless pit.
When a cowboy's home is threatened I can't believe he would just give up and quit.
Amarillo by morning, to enter a rodeo gate,
Does a cowboy sneak in now so a drive-by won't be his fate?
The wild west was no match for a cowboy's grit,
But with gangs and drugs he can't control the bit.
So I very sadly went back to my car,
And told my heart there were no real cowboys anymore.

It's Your Job to Raise Us

There's a mother who cries all through the night,
And a father who says, "This just isn't right."
We're not perfect, but we set a good example.
The needs we provided were more than ample.
He dressed a little strange, but it was just a fad.
When he got that tattoo, we did get mad.
Maybe we should have asked about drugs.
I asked him once, all he did was shrug.
It's just a freak thing he ran into,
I got tired of hearing, "It can happen to you."
Everyone blows crime way out of proportion.
It's a politician's tactic to win with distortion.
The police brought him home a dozen times.
He wasn't doing anything, they just wanted the fines.
Now we have to bury him because he OD'd,
And all the ones, responsible, get off scot-free.
The schools, the police, what do we pay taxes for?
It's their job to watch them once they leave out, our door.
If they would spend more time going after the crooks,
They could catch them all, and our kids wouldn't get hooked.
I'm going to vote "NO" on more prisons and cops,
Until they do something to see this crime wave stops.
"Mom, Dad, you always said, it's your job to raise us,
And wherever we are, we have to merit your trust.
If you thought my brother was in so much danger,
Why did you let him go out with that stranger?
If us kids, can't trust our parents to guide us through,
Then when you say you care, that just isn't true.
When we came to you with any thing, but problems to achieve,
You would blame somebody else or just wouldn't believe."

My Dream

The trees were high
And dripping with dew.
In a circle, above the sky
Was clear and blue.
I was in the mountains, but
I was asleep.
The only sound
Was pure and sweet.
A line with cloths
So white,
They put to shame
The morning light.
And big round flowers
As white as snow,
The aroma filled the air with a peaceful glow.
My eyes lifted up and
I awoke.
This is paradise,
My mind spoke.

I dreamed this about my birth place, Park City, Utah.

A Lifetime Trip

I've been through forever, and back again.
It's a journey to somewhere cause somewhere's at the end.
More sky than land, the wind blows a lot.
Imaginary waves rising from a vapor mirage when it's hot.
Railroad tracks that are close or in a distant haze,
On them trains, always going both ways.
On both sides of the middle of the road,
In a line beyond vision are electric and telephone poles.
The travelers are some you envy and pity,
A whole lot spend most of their time in the city.
Going up and down mountains can take forever,
Or crossing the prairie or ocean in cold or hot weather.
Forever can be a lifetime trip,
Unless you or someone else makes a fatal slip.
Going around forever in a circle, or one spot on earth,
Wondering what forever means from our moment of
birth.
One can hear two beliefs spoken by the ignorant,
And the clever.
"Nothing lasts forever" or "It will last forever."

Joe said to me, "Grandma,
I wish there was a
Magic potion
You could drop on the land
And in the ocean.
Then everyone would love each other
No one would fight, not even
Sister and brother.
Why doesn't God make everyone be good,
And see that all the world has lots of food?"

(And I replied)

"My precious child, we all
Wish that were true,
But God in His wisdom
Left peace up to
Me and you."

God's Gift

My darling Karen, with freckles of gold.
Treasures of faith, your mind abundantly holds.
Every little deed or great big chore you do
Is an act of faith God gave to you.
When you see a human who claims he has God's gift.
For only one to possess is a myth.
A healer can heal you if you think he can,
But your infliction could be part of God's plan.
God might weep because you didn't endure,
You turned from God and went to man for a cure.
God uses pain and grief for a tool
To guide and teach you on Earth's school.
These tools God supplies you when it's time to reap.
When you are puzzled or lost, it isn't man you should seek.
Glory is God's. He is your Saviour.
No man should alter or stop God's behavior.
When you need help, let God take control.
Only He and you can save your soul.
You know God is real. Don't let go of His hand.
He could feel deserted if you take your problems to a mortal man.
Sooner or later, the man won't be there.
Then what will you do when you need someone to care.
You will get on your knees and say, "God, I have returned
To the one who is eternal, this lesson I have learned."

The Path to God

First an atheistic home against God, there is fury,
Next a guru that only made me weary.

In college a massive dose of LSD
Was false communication to the path to Eternity.

Join my church, and do what I say,
When you want something, forget God, to me pray.

The congregation emitting undeserved pride,
They are Gods' only when they testify.

But even their own are shunned and rejected,
When the belief of man they unknowingly neglected.

Life is a play, that God wrote, using faith to direct
Our performance on stage will portray the effect.

Will we give glory to the Author without a pause,
Or will we falter and try to claim the applause?

Enter the farmer with mud on his shoes, or the hippie with long hair.
Enter the poor, with ragged clothes, or the prostitute, almost bare.

Enter the millionaire who stands to the far right, and the judgmental join him to protest.
On the left and the right, all gather to be blessed.

The minister looks sadly over his flock,
As he clears his throat and tries to talk.

The door opens wide, and enters a radiant light
That floods the chapel on the left, middle, and the far right.

The left side and middle absorb and are warmed with Gods' love.
The far right side is blinded and ashamed to look above.

How many times, when the end is near,
We turn to God, because of mortal fear?
We beg God to let us remain with the living,
We can count the times he did, but not the time he stopped forgiving.

Fishing the Red

Fishing the Red, when it recedes
Involves red mud up to your knees.

Slipping and sliding to get to the bank.
Sat on my chair and in the mud it sank.

Got my pole fixed up and threw it in.
Went to reel it tight, it was stuck on a limb.

The tackle box was still in the truck.
I guess that was dumb, not just bad luck.

I trudged on back through the mud and grime,
Knowing when I returned I'd catch one this time.

After a few no nibble hours
The mud dried up and the worms lost their power.

The lazy old river just meandered by,
And the sun was fading through the hole in the sky.

I guess I'll never get my wish.
To catch a great big catfish.

I'll just eat and smoke, and think up a tale.
The one that got away was as big as a whale.

Poems

Poems are feelings
Recorded and preserved.
When life is a standoff,
We need a reserve.
Poems are to satisfy
The curious mind
When it wonders if life
Corresponds with time.
Even a child understands all
When explained in rhyme.

After every war, the next two generations carry on bitterness that they know nothing about. Sometimes the parents and grandparents tell them to forget the past, it's over, and get on with life. Unless it is something that is still going on, we must work on a good future and not dwell on the past.

The Generation Who Has No Claim

On what happened to your parents, why do you dwell?
You're listening to where pity lives, your parents' hearts
are well.
Your parents accepted the natural and forgot the pain.
To their memories of yesterday you have no claim.
You can't accept the necessities and mistakes of history.
When told to you by a few, you believe only the misery.
My anger is aimed at the injustice of war,
And the ones who continue to open the sore.
From the beginning of time, to the very end,
Wars will rage on by foe or friend.
It doesn't matter by whom we are captured or freed.
What matters is why the world keeps repeating this deed.

Little Child

Little child, with skin so dark,
Tell me what is in your heart.
"Mommy's smile, Daddy's love, God's grace,
And courage and determination because of my race."

Little child who has yellow skin,
What in life do you need to win?
"Mommy's help, Daddy's love, God's grace,
And the world to accept me in any place."

Little child with a natural red glow,
What about life do you need to know?
"My mommy, Daddy's love, God's grace,
And to always lead me, my ancestor's face."

Little child, your body is brown.
Your passage through life, where is it found?
"Mommy's words, Daddy's love, God's grace,
And the long ago wisdom of Spanish lace."

Little child, you were born white.
What do you need to have a good life?
"Mommy's care, Daddy's love, God's grace,
And every color and hue in my flower vase."

I Live on the Street

I live on the street. My home's in my heart.
Most of the time, I sleep in the park.
I just had bad luck. I don't do crime.
Some real bad dudes are here all the time.

I was always careful to show respect,
So humanity I would always reflect.
I walked right up and said, "Hey you guys,
I heard you telling the police those lies."

"We are not animals. We are human beings.
I'd like my neighbors to keep it clean.
I know what the police were asking you about.
You were breaking the law, and there's no doubt."

I may live on the street, but I abide by the law.
I want to hold my head proudly to all.
If I lived in a mansion, it wouldn't matter.
I am an American citizen, and nothing makes me sadder
Than to see anyone tear this country apart.
They are destroying my home because that's in my heart.

On the Words of a Poem

I was young and restless for what life had in store,
I started seeking every nook and cranny, every forbidden door.
Every new horizon rose up, and beckoned me to explore.

When I married, I thought I would be free, to act my own
way, with no demands on me.
In a very short time, I learned that wasn't to be.

When I had my own kids, I would tell them what to do,
But they were in control, even when brand new.
Feeding, crying, changing diapers, I was never so blue.

I'd get a job that was glamorous and fun,
And I'd leave the kids, with some other one.
I'd live the dream life when I was done.

Needless to say, that didn't work out.
I was head cook at a school where the staff and kids, were
prone to pout.
I could stay at home to hear the population scream and shout.

My kids finally grew up, all safe and sound,
Some scrapes and bruises, some ups and downs.
But before I recovered, grandkids all around.

I've been told many times, "Your life's not your own."
Once you leave, you keep trying to go back home.
Almost giving up, I found the way, On the Words of a Poem.

Lost Years

Long lost years of yesterday,
Gone past my eyes, forever.
Gone on your own mournful way,
Leaving my cares to endeavor.

I was a king, mighty and bold,
Stronger than many a man.
But I would have given it all
For just one honest friend.

Someone who's there, joy or fear,
Beside me through life,
Just to have brought Heaven near,
A friend, a woman, a wife.

Written at the age of seventeen.

Sweet Refrain

A peace I've found,
I know not why.
It makes no sound,
No whimper or cry.
It fills the air
With sweet refrain.
All seems fair,
With all to gain.
The time is short
And will not stay,
But in my heart
I will not forget this day.
The search goes on.
I'll never find,
What has gone,
This peace of mind.

I Walked with My Love

One day so sweet,
He talked of nature's
Beauty and listened
To songs the birds
Repeat.
He laughed with the wind
And praised the sky, and
Loved the colors in the
Butterfly.
He told of the tree
That grew so tall, And
Drank in all the beauty of the
Waterfall.
I listened closely and
Tried to understand, All
He could see in this fair
Land.
But yet my heart was not
Quite well, It remembered
Only the things he did
Not tell.

Does Love Last Forever?

Does love last forever with many phases?
Can it survive in silence without any praises?

Will you stay forever when you know you should go,
Constantly alert, so your hurt won't show?

Can you really never make a mistake?
All that you are, to please, you forsake.

Is there enough in-between the loneliness
To keep you there, tending the nest.

Can you live a life, you're never sure,
Somewhere else, you would be wanted more?

You get angry and cry, and swear it's the end.
You pack and you leave, just to come back again.

When you leave, feelings of panic and fear
Bring you back to where hope is near.

The other one might change his mind.
Or be sorry for words that were unkind.

No matter how bad things might be,
When you refer to life, you want to say "we."

What is the reason you can't walk away?
Is it your mind or your heart that makes you stay?

Which force, is greater, out of the two?
I've lived a long time, and haven't a clue.

Is my love as real as when we first met?
Or does my mind subdue some regret?

They always say love borders on hate.
Maybe that means, accept your fate.

You want to love, but you want to know
Your mate is a friend, and not a foe.

They say you're lucky to come so far.
Luck didn't get us where we are.

So many times the end was in sight,
Then through the mist, the tiniest light.

Then a little hope, it won't be over today.
Time will heal, so why not stay.

Is it love or habit, you don't want to lose?
Is your mind or your heart too tired to choose?

I don't even know why I stayed so long.
Because I loved, or just wanted to belong.

When someone tells you they want to be free
And you cry and beg, please stay with me.

But he won't budge, so you start to pack.
You know it's over and accept that fact.

All of a sudden, you can stay if you change.
Leave him alone, and his life don't arrange.

I wanted him still, so I swallowed my pride,
And buried my love way deep inside.

Whenever it surfaced, I soon learned,
What he did was none of my concern.

Looks of pure hate and words that revealed,
His bad feelings for me had never healed.

The only thing I can read in his eyes, and his voice
I stayed out of duty, I had no choice.

He gave his word, but he couldn't hide,
His love for me had completely died.

What I did wrong has never been clear.
He just no longer wanted me near.

So both of our lives have been wasted, I guess.
But I want you to know I did my best.

That Old Famous Saying

There is a saying in the world that has complete control,
To determine the ego, intellect of the young and old.

The saying is as old as time, after humans appeared,
Maybe before, but we don't know how animals are reared.

Once it's uttered the subject's life that's arranged.
In spite of the saying, some turn out strange.

There is a pattern instilled in every developed mind, and
For hundreds of years to rebel is a mortal crime.

It's hard to believe that a saying is true,
Can suggest so strongly the respect that is due.

History books, *The Bible,* human strength, originated the ego saying.
Nothing has changed its eternal power, not crying or praying.

Some have tried and won a few battles, but
It's like being in a rowboat without any paddles.

You're in the middle of the lake, safe and dry in the boat.
You'll never get to shore, just sit there and float.

You can be helped if you ask the subject the saying pertains to,
But only if the subject has a mind or heart that will help you.

The saying effects some with fear, some with awe, some with joy.
That famous old saying, "HONEY, IT'S A BOY!"

The Junction

Neither Christian, Atheist, or God can claim as their own,
The actions, values, thoughts, that abide in a fair moral home.

Anyone who lives and teaches an example, bad or good,
And most of all shows respect for each neighborhood,
Are the ones who lay the foundation
For a peaceful, caring, loving nation.

Schools can teach and practice values, without using religion.
Personnel Preference and One's God is a home and not a school decision.

To teach in school *The Bible*, or the beginning of man and earth,
Or if or if not to give birth, is not a school function.
A school is in the middle of the beginning and the end,
it's called a Junction.

The Junction should be peaceful, fair, and enforce the Golden Rule.
Reading, writing, arithmetic, basic history, respect, is the reason for school.

If while in school someone should slip and say, "Amen,"
An understanding smile, then silence from an Atheist friend.
Then the first to speak, should realize, his word might offend.

Then the two together should get on with the school function,
So they are capable of choosing their right path out of the Junction.